DEMCO

Why Why Why are sharks so scary?

MC
PUBLISHERS

First published as hardback in 2006 by Miles Kelly Publishing Ltd, Bardfield Centre, Great Bardfield, Essex, CM7 4SLCopyright
© Miles Kelly Publishing Ltd 2006

This 2009 edition published and distributed by:

Mason Crest Publishers Inc.
370 Reed Road, Broomall, Pennsylvania 19008
(866) MCP-BOOK (toll free)
www.masoncrest.com

Why Why Why—
Are Sharks So Scary?
ISBN 978-1-4222-1571-5
Library of Congress Cataloging-in-Publication data is available

Why Why Why—?
Complete 23 Title Series
ISBN 978-1-4222-1568-5

Printed in the United States of America

Contents

What is a shark?

Blue shark

A shark is a meat-eating fish that lives in the sea. All sharks have a strong sense of smell to help them find their prey — the animals they hunt for food. Most sharks have a big mouth and sharp teeth.

Whale shark

Shark submarines!

Most submarines can dive to about 1,000 feet, but the Portuguese shark can dive down to 12,000 feet.

Where in the world do sharks live?

Sharks live in seas and oceans around the world. They are often found by the coast, a few miles from the beach. Each type of shark has its own favorite place to live.

Great white shark

Starry smooth-hound shark

Basking shark

Sandbar shark

How many types of shark are there?

There are around 330 kinds of shark. The most common is the blue shark. Each type of shark is different in size, color and markings. Types of shark can also behave differently.

Draw

Sketch a scary shark with big teeth chasing small fish in the sea.

How does a shark swim?

A shark swims by using its fins. The tail itself is a fin, and moves from side to side using strong muscles to push the shark through the water. The fin on the top of the body is called the dorsal fin. This keeps the shark upright in the water.

Shark cookies!

The cookie-cutter shark was given its name because of how it feeds. It bites its prey and then swivels its sharp teeth in a circle to cut away a cookie-shaped lump of flesh.

How does a shark breathe?

A shark breathes through its gills, which are slits on the sides of its head. Most sharks have to keep swimming all the time so that water is always flowing over their gills, allowing them to breathe.

Dorsal fin

Gills

Play

Sharks have good night-time eyesight. When you next go to bed, see how well you can see in the dark.

Do sharks have good senses?

Yes! Sharks can see well even at night, and can smell blood from miles away. Hearing is not their best sense, but they can still hear scuba divers breathing. Their ears are tiny holes just behind their eyes.

Why do sharks have pointy teeth?

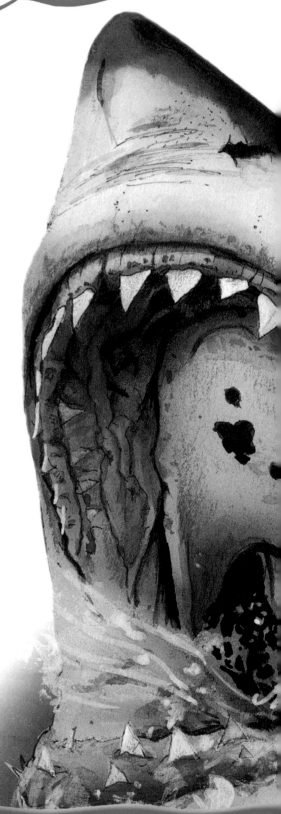

So they can saw lumps of flesh off the animals they catch! The teeth are narrow with sharp areas along their edges. The great white shark's teeth grow almost 3 inches in length — that's about the size of your middle finger.

Do sharks go to sleep?

Most sharks don't sleep. However, whale sharks sometimes stop swimming to rest on the seabed. They can stay still like this for months. This helps them save energy when there is not much food.

Sneaky shark!

The blind shark of Australia isn't blind at all! It has thick eyelids that when shut, make the shark look blind.

Tiger shark

What do sharks eat?

Sharks eat all kinds of meat, including fish and seals. Some sharks hunt and chase their prey, or feast on dying or dead animals. Other sharks lie in wait for food, and some swim open-mouthed to swallow small prey in the water.

Great white shark

Count

Whale sharks can stay still in the water for months. Time how long you can stay still for.

Do sharks lay eggs?

Some sharks do lay eggs, but others give birth to live babies. A shark egg contains the young shark and a yolk. The yolk feeds the shark until it hatches. An empty egg case is called a 'mermaid's purse'.

50 days

100 days

Egg

Think

Sharks are not the only animals that lay eggs. How many egg-laying animals can you think of?

Do sharks look after their babies?

No they don't. As soon as they are born, baby sharks have to look after themselves. They have to hunt for their own food and protect themselves against other creatures that try to eat them.

Hungry pups!

As the young of the sand tiger shark grow inside their mother, the biggest one with the most developed teeth may feed on the smaller, weaker ones.

150 days

200 days

Pup developing in an egg

250 days

Shark pup

What are baby sharks called?

Baby sharks are called pups. They normally look like smaller versions of their parents, but have brighter colors and markings. Many pups get eaten, as they are easy prey for dolphins, sea lions and other sharks.

Which shark has a very long tail?

The thresher shark does. Its tail can measure up to 10 feet in length – that's almost as long as a car! Threshers use their tails to slap and bash smaller fish before swallowing them. Other sharks hit the top of the water with their tails to scare fish.

Thresher shark

Pretend

Imagine you're an epaulette shark. Use your elbows and knees as fins. Can you walk?

Can a shark walk?

An epaulette shark can. This shark uses its strong fins like arms to drag itself onto dry land. This way it can travel along the seashore from one rock pool to the next.

Epaulette shark

How do sharks hide in water?

A shark's coloring can help to disguise it. Sharks often have dark backs, which help them blend into the dark waters below. They are a paler color underneath, allowing them to blend in with the light at the water's surface.

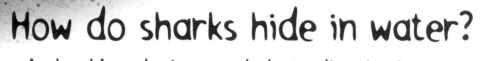

Mega shark!

The biggest shark ever was probably *Megalodon*. It lived millons of years ago, and grew up to 65 feet in length — three times bigger than today's great white shark.

Can sharks be goblins?

Yes they can! Goblin sharks are bright pink and have long, pointy noses to help them find food. They are rarely caught by humans, so little is known about them. Scientists think they grow to 12 feet in length, which is a bit longer than a car.

Giant teeth!

Scientists have discovered teeth from giant prehistoric sharks that are as big as an adult's hand!

Are sharks slimy?

Most sharks have very slimy skin. The slime helps them to move smoothly through the water, but it is worn away as they swim. Luckily sharks are able to make lots of new slime very quickly!

Goblin shark

Make

Fold a strip of paper several times to make a concertina shape. Now you have your own frilly collar!

Why are some sharks frilly?

The frilled shark has six gills, so it looks like it's wearing a frilly collar. Most sharks only have five gills. It also has special teeth — each tooth has three points — perfect for grabbing octopus, one of its favorite foods.

Frilled shark

Which shark can disappear?

An angel shark can. Its wide, flat body is sand-colored so it blends perfectly with the seabed. These sharks are called angel sharks because their fins spread out wide like an angel's wings. They can lie in wait for over a week until the right food comes along.

Angel shark

Hide

See if you can blend into your surroundings like an angel shark. Can anyone find you?

How do sharks find mates?

They use their sense of smell! When it's time to make babies, sharks give off special smells into the water to attract one another. Some sharks don't mate very often, and can become rare.

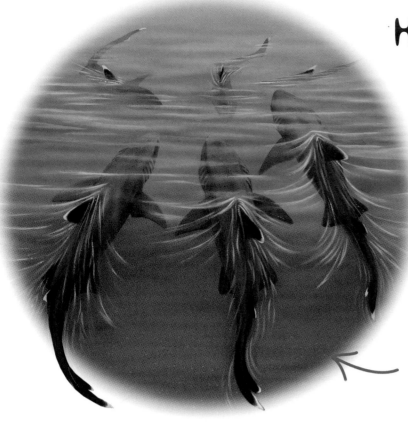

White-tip reef sharks

Do sharks have cousins?

Yes, they do – in a way. Sharks have close relatives such as skates and rays. The bodies of these fish are similar to those of sharks. Stingrays have sharp spines on their tails. These contain poison that they stab into prey, or any creatures that try to attack them.

Greedy shark!

A dead greenland shark was once found with a whole reindeer in its stomach! These sharks usually eat fish and squid, but they have been known to eat dead whales.

Which fish stick to sharks?

Fish called sharksuckers do! Using a ridged sucker on their heads, they stick onto large sharks so they don't have to swim, and can go wherever the shark goes. When the shark finds a meal, the sharksucker can break off and steal what food is left.

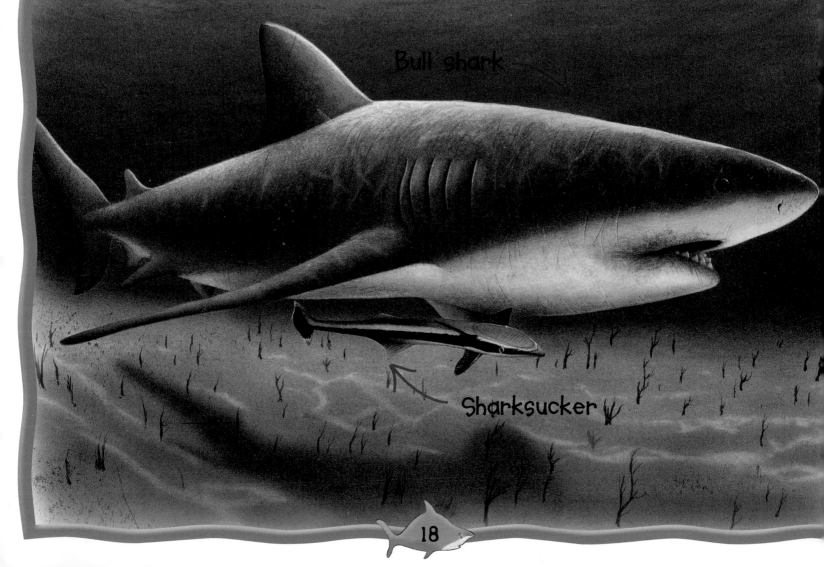

Bull shark

Sharksucker

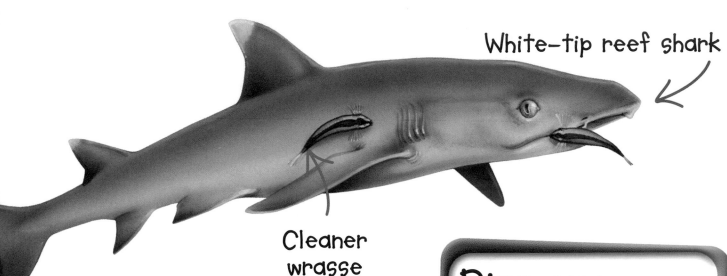

White-tip reef shark

Cleaner wrasse

Do sharks have friends?

Sharks and cleaner wrasse fish help each other. Sharks even let these fish into their mouths without eating them. The cleaner wrasse eat the dirt on the shark's teeth, and in return the shark gets its teeth cleaned.

Discover

Blue sharks swim across the Atlantic Ocean from the Caribbean to western Europe. Find these places on an atlas.

Glowing sharks!

Lanternsharks can glow in the dark. The light they create attracts small creatures such as fish and squid, so the shark can snap them up.

Do sharks lose their teeth?

Yes – most shark's teeth are quite narrow and can snap off. New teeth are always growing to replace any that are lost. Some sharks lose over 3000 teeth in their lifetime.

Which shark is as big as a whale?

The whale shark is. In fact it is the biggest shark of all. It can grow to be as long as five cars – that's 60 feet in length. Whale sharks can weigh more than 12 tons – that's the same weight as 12 large horses.

Whale shark

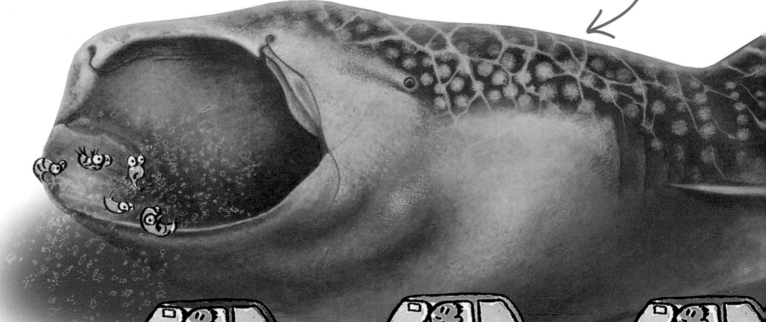

 Saw shark

Which shark digs for its dinner?

The saw shark does! Its long nose is surrounded by teeth, so it looks like a saw. They use their noses to dig up prey from the seabed. Then they slash and tear at the food.

Dinner time!

Krill look like small shrimps and are about 1 inch in length. Whale sharks feed by taking water into their mouths and trapping krill before swallowing them.

Find out

Use the Internet or books to find information and pictures about krill. Where do they live?

Why are sharks so scary?

Sharks seem scary because they are so big and have sharp teeth. We feel unable to protect ourselves against them. Sharks are often shown in films and on television as more dangerous than they really are.

Which shark wears a disguise?

The wobbegong shark seems to. However, its lumpy body, with patterns and bumps, is what actually makes it look just like rocks and seaweed. It also has a wide, flat body to help it hide on the seabed. A wobbegong will wait for fish to swim past and then gobble them up.

Wobbegong shark

Shark enemies!

Even sharks have enemies. Large, powerful sharks such as hammerheads are attacked by elephant seals, which can weigh up to 5 tons.

What is the fastest shark?

The mako shark is. It can swim at more than 35 miles per hour. It is speedy because of its slim shape. The mako can also jump well, leaping up to 33 feet out of the water.

Mako shark

Which shark will eat anything?

Tiger sharks are the least fussy eaters. They have been known to eat all kinds of strange things – bottles, tools, car tires, and in one case, even a type of drum called a tom-tom!

Remember

From what you have read, can you remember which sharks like to live on the seabed?

Can small sharks be fierce?

They can when they hunt in a group. Pygmy sharks are one of the smallest types of shark, at only 7 to 8 inches in length. By working together they can attack and kill fish much larger than themselves. Luckily, pygmy sharks are harmless to humans.

Pygmy sharks

Think

If you had discovered the megamouth shark what would you have called it? What other shark names can you think of?

Do sharks use hammers?

A hammerhead does! Its hammer-shaped head gives it a better sense of smell. This is because its nostrils are far apart, one on each side of its head. This helps the hammerhead to find out quickly where a smell is coming from, so it can track down its food.

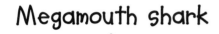
Megamouth shark

Tiny sharks!

The smallest sharks could lie curled up in your hand. The dwarf lanternshark is just 6 inches in length.

Which shark is a big-mouth?

The megamouth shark's mouth is more than 4 feet in width. Inside are rows of tiny teeth. This shark swims through shoals of fish with its mouth wide open, trapping and swallowing its prey.

Can sharks be prickly?

Yes they can! Most sharks have tough, slightly spiky skin. The bramble shark is a deep-water shark that has very prickly skin. It is covered in large, sharp thorn-like spikes that act as protection from predators.

Bramble shark

Hot sharks!

Unlike most sharks, great whites are partly warm-blooded. This helps the muscles in their bodies work better, allowing them to swim quickly when hunting.

When is a shark like a zebra?

When it is young, a zebra shark is covered in stripes. It has dark and pale stripes that run along its body. As it gets older it grows up to 10 feet in length, and its stripes separate, turning into spots.

Adult zebra shark

Draw

Design a poster to show why we need to look after sharks, and how people can help.

Do sharks eat people?

Sharks very rarely eat people. If they do attack, it's because they think we are prey, or because they are hungry. Most people survive shark attacks, because once sharks realize the person is not their usual food, they leave them alone.

Are all sharks dangerous?

No, most sharks are harmless. However some sharks such as the great white, tiger and bull shark have been known to attack people. These sharks are always on the look-out for food, which is why they can be dangerous.

Count

Now you have read this book, how many different kinds of shark can you remember?

A great white shark

Do people eat sharks?

Some people do. In places such as Asia, shark fin soup is very popular. People hunting sharks for food has led to some sharks becoming very rare. We need to protect sharks or they may die out forever.

Shark watching!

Some people go on trips in glass-bottomed boats to see sharks. This doesn't upset the sharks, and it allows people to understand them better.

How can we learn about sharks?

Scientists can learn about sharks by watching them in the wild. This can be dangerous if the sharks are hungry, or come too close. To stay safe, people watch sharks from inside diving cages where they can't get hurt.

Quiz time

Do you remember what you have read about sharks?

These questions will test your memory. The pictures will help you. If you get stuck, read the pages again.

3. Do sharks go to sleep?

page 8

page 11

4. Do sharks look after their babies?

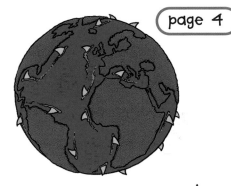

page 4

1. Where in the world do sharks live?

page 12

5. Which shark has a very long tail?

page 7

2. How does a shark breathe?

page 14

6. Are sharks slimy?

7. How do sharks find mates?

page 17

page 24

11. Can small sharks be fierce?

8. Do sharks lose their teeth?

page 27

12. Do sharks eat people?

page 19

page 29

page 21

9. Which shark digs for its dinner?

13. How can we learn about sharks?

page 23

10. Which shark will eat anything?

Answers

1. In seas and oceans around the world
2. Through its gills
3. Most sharks don't sleep
4. No, they don't
5. The thresher shark
6. Most sharks have very slimy skin
7. By using their noses!
8. Yes — they sometimes snap off
9. The saw shark
10. The tiger shark
11. Yes, if they hunt in a group
12. Yes, but very rarely
13. By watching them in the wild

Index